One Perspective from the End of the World

BY

MYAH

ROBBINS

atmosphere press

Published by Atmosphere Press

Illustrations and cover design by Debbie Hottle

atmospherepress.com

TABLE OF CONTENTS

INTERMISSION

DARKER DAYS

EPILOGUE

BRIGHT OUTLOOK

"Measure the skies, and range the realms above.
There in one view we grasp the mighty whole,
Or with new worlds amaze th' unbounded soul."

—On Imagination, Phillis Wheatley

ON OPTIMISM

Sometimes I look up and see the stars

So close

I could grasp them in my hand

Sometimes I look up and see the sky

Tinted pink

To mark day's end

But sometimes I look up to see a storm

Rolling in

Overhead

Say

What if the stars

And the sky

Were just

A murky trick of the eye

Maybe the bravest thing someone can do

Is look up

And hope for starshine

A MOMENT

The sun shines down on us today

With a sunset filter

Of pink and blue and purple and gray

Soon even that will fade

Leaving only the moon shining on

With a rainbow halo

Forming a crown

You, a bystander

Watch these moments come

So one day you'll remember them

Many years from now

Your feet sink into the sand

The wind ruffles your hair

The cold might bite

Or the heat might sting

But for the moment

In the moment

Your mind roams nowhere else

But there

SEA TRINKETS

Trinkets of the sea

Scatter on the shore

Sent by the waves

Under

A layer of seafoam

A seashell painting

Of lovely little blues

Calls of calm things

With light little hues

Next is a sand dollar

Smoldering[1] with luck

Grasped nicely in your hand

A charm you've amassed[2]

Such are seashells

So different in meaning

In each of our feelings

So many listless little pretty things

---

[1] Smoldering: burning of an intense feeling or thing
[2] Amassed: collected

For us

To find

Each person an interpreter

Each shell

A cipher

All work of art

In their own right

THE UNKNOWN

Let's embark[3]

To the enchanted forest

Say

I see

Magic in the air

And a bridge

Off into

The unknown

So tempting to take

But I'll never be sure

If I can return

Until

I go

Let's breathe in this day

And embark

Off into

The unknown

---

[3] Embark: depart to/leave to

EXHILARATION

I see lightning's flashing light

Jolting[4] my every bone

I see swirling clouds

Whispering impending[5] doom

But I'm not scared

As I ride, my reigns hung slack

Racing as the thunder blares

So I can grab the stars from the sky

You'd wish forever was your calm

But maybe

I rather like the storm

---

[4] Jolting: shocking someone or something with surprise
[5] Impending: describes something about to happen

CLOUD COLORS

The fog is growing denser

And all I see are clouds

White for our calm days

Gray of foreboding haze

Misty for nostalgic[6] bouts[7]

And ones where

You can't see anything

At all

Tell me

When did light become so surreal[8]?

---

[6] Nostalgic: remembering something of the past affectionately
[7] Bout: a small period of time for an intense activity
[8] Surreal: a strange feeling, almost dream-like

LOOKING UP

I found myself one day

Looking down

And I showed all I had

Worth looking up for

I saw your golden hair

I heard your harmonica sing

I tasted Hard Work's end

And I felt your crooked grin

After all

It's all the little simple things

Scattered through infinity

That really

Truly

Gives our life its meaning

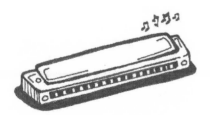

MASKED

Darkness fell, pandemic dawned

You cannot silence the people, their call

For resilience[9]

We'll be resilient

For together we stand, together we fall

But if that's true

Then where

Where have all the people gone?

Some cover their faces

But choose to ignore

All those who had covered

Their faces before

What happened to rainbows

A colorful world

If you see in black and white, I'm sorry

For love is a rainbow

You'll never see

---

[9] Resilience: the ability to recover from things/how tough you are

Plagued or no

A disease is spreading

It takes a man, a woman, a child

Who is brave

To disrupt the chaos and say

This is no way to save

We the people

Are deranged[10]

We the people

Need to come together

And act

Just a little bit

Sane

We're losing our heads

Resilience is a joke

We need to put our heads together

Do the hardest thing:

Hope

---

[10] Deranged: very wrong and off in some way

We're all masked

And when masks are null[11]

I'm not sure I'll be able

To recognize myself

Anymore

We're all masked

But underneath

I want to be proud of my peers

The people

We the people

To have begun to defeat

The insurmountable[12] disease

Encompassing[13] our world

---

[11] Null: nothing/gone/zero
[12] Insurmountable: unable to be overcome or beaten
[13] Encompassing: covering/spreading around

CHRISTMAS POEMS

"Year's end is neither an end nor a beginning
but a going on, with all the wisdom
that experience can instill in us."

–Hal Borland

GNOME CHRISTMAS

A gnome's favorite holiday is Christmas

Ever dare to wonder why

For one would never brave to think otherwise

With those hats they ever like

MERRY CHRISTMAS

Merry Christmas

Merry Christmas

This year

Let's all be joyful

We may not be gleeful[14]

But we'll all be hopeful

For better days

This year

Let's leave it all be

For now

We'll all be okay

For now

And let's have a merry

Let's have a

Merry Christmas

This year

[14] Gleeful: with loads of joy

SING-ALONG

Deck the halls

With jolly

Our song sleighs away

Oh what fun

It is to plagiarize

My Christmas poem away

Let's wear

Happy clothes

And sing

Our Yuletide[15] carols

To waste our days away

Till next year folks

Let's just

Deem[16] to hope

It'll greet us

With better days

Better Days...

---

[15] Yuletide: an aged word for
    Christmas
[16] Deem: decide

BLESS THE SIMPLE THINGS

What is Christmas?

In your hearts

Let's skip the sappy[17]

And try

The true part

I saw a smile today

I heard my violin sing

The aroma of cookies

Entered my den

And I felt

Slightly normal again

I say

Christmas is

To bless the simple things

For where would we be

If each task was hard

And we lacked the space to breathe

[17] Sappy: describes something that's cheesy and heartwarming

I'll cry

Let's bless the simple things

And slow down

To enjoy the ride

Downhill

As it may be

SKELETON TREE

Season's greetings

My friend

We'll spend our days cavorting[18]

Under the shining star of Bethlehem

It seems forever and now too soon

Our ever-approaching winter begins

To mark year's coming end

My pen bleeds down the paper

Pine prickling my skin

Spirits dropped and singing stopped

Under a veil[19] of glowing gloom

Revealing

The most underwhelming Christmas of all

A skeleton tree

To mark the season's end

---

[18] Cavorting: dancing
[19] Veil: a covering/something that covers

COUNTDOWN

Five days

Four days

Now it's

Three

A countdown

To Christmas

In me

Countdowns

Click

Inside me

A countdown

To madness

A countdown

To loss

Of

My sanity

But loudest

Thank God

Is the countdown to Christmas

Clanging loudly

Of joyful preach[20]

---

[20] Preach: pray for something

MY HEAD

My head

Pounds

With madness

I can't write

In a state

Such as this

Where is

My Christmas spirit

I want to close my eyes

And sleep till

2021

CHRISTMAS SPIRIT

Christmas spirit

Or lack thereof

Is really getting on my nerves

If I write more

Then I'll complain

And we've no time

For useless words

When there's a whole wide world

To explore

Or not

Let's not

I'm in no mood to hurl[21]

Should I digress[22]

If it was in sickness

Or at the decrepit[23]

State of the world

---

[21] Hurl: to barf/to throw up
[22] Digress: to move away from the main subject
[23] Decrepit: lousy/bad

A DAY OF REDS AND GREENS

What color is Christmas

What clouds your vision

Each and every

Holiday

Christmas is

A day of reds and greens

Tinted white

By the snow

A day for jolly

Joyful peace

To make our days

Worthwhile

So why when I sit

Entranced[24] by song

Does Christmas feel

Oh so blue

This year

---

[24] Entranced: to fill a person with wonder and catch their attention fully

BRIGHT LIGHTS

Bright lights

On a dark night

Shine into view

Such brightness

And lightness

These days

Are something new

They burn my eyes

Let's embrace[25] to darkness's

Enveloping[26] soothe[27]

---

[25] Embrace: to hold closely
[26] Enveloping: to cover fully
[27] Soothe: to calm someone

SILENT NIGHT

A somber[28] song strikes me

And carries me away

Whilst[29] carols fail

To entrance me

My lonesome[30] spirit fades

Yes the nights are silent

But who said silence

Was oh so bright

Sleep in heavenly peace

Let's ward[31] the dark away

Sleep in heavenly peace

And hope

For better days

---

[28] Somber: sorrowful/with sadness
[29] Whilst: old word for while
[30] Lonesome: lonely
[31] Ward: to guard/to protect

FOOD FOR THOUGHT

*"Dreaming is like a light hanging off a chandelier
and twirling around."*

–Phaedra Robbins

DÉJÀ VU THE FIRST

Sometimes I wake

To swirling déjà vu

Hindering[32] my day

It seems

I've done this all

Before

Deep breaths I'll take

I've heard of nostalgia

But this is all

So much

More

Sometimes I wake

To roiling[33] déjà vu

It seems

I've done this all

Before

---

[32] Hindering: slowing
[33] Roiling: annoying/irritating

A YELLOW WORLD

My world once was yellow

Plagued with dark black spots

Nothing's changed since then

Except, perhaps

My perception

Life goes on, though

What can one say more?

After all

Ignorance is bliss[34]

'Cause ever since

I've lost my trust in yellow

---

[34] Bliss: joy to the highest degree

DREAM

Head in the clouds

A listless train of thought

Reality forsakes[35] me

Again

---

[35] Forsakes: abandons/leaves behind

CHOOSING SIDES

Wouldn't we be lying

Saying the world doesn't choose a side

I doubt it's mere[36] coincidence

Its pressures on our life

Because

Haven't you ever seen

The trees curling in

To lend a helping hand

Haven't you ever felt

The wind pushing us along

Hasn't there ever been a storm

Where it's quite the strife[37]

To stay alive

Haven't you ever been

Overwhelmed by it all

I guess it's just

---

[36] Mere: no bigger than/just
[37] Strife: trouble/hardship

A matter of time

Before we find

Whose side we're on

FELLOW FIEND

Friend or foe[38]

Fiend[39] or fellow[40]

Such migrants begone

You do not belong

Here

But take me with you

For a sojourner's[41] call

Has lifted off

Within me

Come on

Shouldn't you all

Join your fellow fiend

---

[38] Foe: enemy
[39] Fiend: something devilish in nature
[40] Fellow: a normal person/a peer
[41] Sojourner: wanderer

THE THING ABOUT HONESTY

There's something in all of us

That keeps us honest

A person or feeling

That calls out the truth

But there's something in all of us

That does the opposite

A person or feeling

Where you'd never be true

For in love would you lie?

In hate be sincere[42]?

At what time in your life

Do your walls appear?

Closing in your heart

To all

But those who hold the key

---

[42] Sincere: truthful

LIE WITHOUT LYING

There are many shades of trust

Enveloped in our world

Faeries[43] can't lie

But they shine of twisted words

There's dry cynicism[44]

Sarcastic remarks

Just plain omission[45]

To trouble yourself

You see

Humanity has conjured

Such a multitude of ways

To lie

Without lying

To ourselves

---

[43] Faeries: another word for fairies
[44] Cynicism: thinking the worst of things/people
[45] Omission: the act of leaving something important out when talking

ENOUGH

The render distance[46] is low today

And mist clings to my face

Recently memories have clogged my mind

And déjà vu's become a friend of mine

But still

Flashes come

So new to me

I see fog against the waves

Seeming of a storm

That will never come

I see waves calmer yet

On a seashell

So smooth

Against my fingertips

I see golden hair

Glinted[47] strawberry red

And pitter-patter feet

---

[46] Render distance: the Minecraft term for how far you can see
[47] Glinted: a reflected shine

Bouncing across the sand

I see a girl of gold and blue

Sleep soundly across the couch

And I see all of you

And I am happy with what I have

Now that's all I see

And it's enough for me   *And it would be*

At least   *Enough for me*

For now   *If it weren't for you*

FAITH

Faith: complete trust in someone or something

Faith

A fickle[48] force that can determine the world

Of God, a deity,[49] heaven divine

Or just of love

Of trust

I *had* that

Everyone starts with

Blind faith

Until someone lets them down

Someone always lets you down

If I have faith

The world will be as bright as the stars

Until

It goes supernova[50]

And all falls apart

I won't begin to question

---

[48] Fickle: unruly/reckless
[49] Deity: a being with god-like amounts of power
[50] Supernova: when a larger star's lifetime ends and it explodes

A matter of religion

When

I am not sure of my faith in you

And certainly not of myself

SUCH A THING AS HOPE

So trivial

Such a thing as hope

What is left of the world

When you've begun to doubt its charm?

What worth is a silver lining

Once the paint peels off?

What use do I have trying

When we're all doomed to fall?

Hope

So trivial

So why

Does it put tears in my eyes?

IRONY

A flicker of a wisp[51]

Out on the horizon

Fetches forgotten petals

Of rosy wedding flowers

Left

As a tribute[52]

To the grave

The days are getting cloudier

But what does that mean?

---

[51] Wisp: a small ghost-like spirit or being
[52] Tribute: offering/an act to show respect

DÉJÀ VU II

Déjà vu

Déjà vu

Nothing's new

Anymore

Déjà vu

Is it true

We've done this all

Before

Repeat

Redo

Re-

Again

Is it possible

For me to die

Of boredom?

It's just over and over

Then and again

Déjà vu

Déjà vu

Nothing's new

Anymore

YOUR PATH

There's a fork in the road

Two ways to go

A decision

That splits your life in two

The strangest things can happen

So be mindful

What you choose

Because there'll always be

That winding[53] path you'll never know

Will you feel filling burning warmth

Or sweet bitter cold

On your life's road?

It's rather intimidating

You see

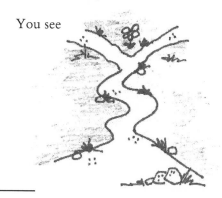

---

[53] Winding: twisting

INTERMISSION

"Pondering is a little like considering and a little like thinking, but looser. To ponder, one must let the facts roll around the rim of the mind's roulette wheel, coming to settle in whichever slot they feel pulled to."

–Christopher Moore

SPELL OF VENGEANCE

Help was once a rich man's friend

Endlessly purchasing means to an end

Lest[54] one forget the servant's hour

Painfully tiring for said rich man's power

Much hurt was gleaned[55] and he tired so

Ever nurturing[56] a grudge's persistent grow

Death was nigh[57] for submission's dream

End for the rich man was yet to glean

Still the servant searched days by the hour

Till finding a relic left to empower

Reality as sanity had left both men

Overwhelmed by pursuit of each dream by then

Yet ever in pursuit of

---

[54] Lest: unless
[55] Gleaned: gained
[56] Nurturing: caring for
[57] Nigh: nothing

53

This thing called vengeance

Headed now to a spell

Imbued[58] with their will

Set now unto the hands of you, for a story anew

A MIRROR

The world dissolves away

All that's left is a man

In a bathroom

With a mirror

Whatever you're imagining, I can assure you,

You are wrong

The man is quite simple, as looks would go

And the bathroom, yet, even more so

But the mirror is the difference

The mirror is the prize

For as the man peers into the mirror

He sees his reflection, yet from behind

What

One would ponder[59]

Could this mirror be?

When you hear the word mirror, you would think

Something quite ordinary

---

[59] Ponder: wonder/think about

But perhaps it's a portal, off into unknown

Where a reflection shows the perspective of not you

But the world from before

Perhaps it's a camera, hidden away

Shown just to trick you of mystical sway[60]

Perhaps it's a mirror, but physics has changed

And what once was shown right

Is now shown deranged

But, then

Alas

A mirror it would not be

For portals and cameras and physics off-course

Is not

Be it not

A real mirror to me

I called it a mirror and it now must be so

But such wonder

We glean

Just from a mirror

Gone wrong

---

[60] Sway: control

DARKER DAYS

"Thus let me live, unseen, unknown;
Thus unlamented let me die;
Steal from the world, and not a stone
Tell where I lie."

—Ode on Solitude, Alexander Pope

UNTITLED

How can I describe to you

A glimpse[61]

A smidgen[62]

A pang[63]

Of how I feel

It's not a picture

Or some words

Not a sound uttered[64]

Portraying[65]

Such a hollow

Heart

'Tis it all

Working together

A symphony

To your ears

To your eyes

---

[61] Glimpse: a small look at something
[62] Smidgen: a little bit
[63] Pang: a sudden, short burst of feeling
[64] Uttered: spoken
[65] Portraying: showing

And your mind

A mellow[66] cacophony[67]

Of atonality[68]

Gibberish epitomized[69]

To all

But those

Unlucky enough

To have felt

What I've been through

Your brain turns against you

Words twisted in your head

Your world burns before you

And you're the only one left

Imagine

A heart

Your heart

As full

As full

---

[66] Mellow: a soft sadness
[67] Cacophony: a harsh mix of noises
[68] Atonality: a sound, usually in song, that doesn't sound full
[69] Epitomized: being the perfect example of something

Can be

Beating

Triumphantly[70]

So beautiful

A world

Full of wonder

But wonder can be twisted too

And that heart

Your heart

Has been ripped

Away

From you

Still beating

Off in the distance

To your ears

And you're left

The last one standing

A shell

Of anything left

---

[70] Triumphantly: in great success

Worth meaning

You're in shambles[71]

Still stumbling

Searching

For what

You had

Before

Ever notice

In the bright autumn leaves

How fake your yellow seems

It's always speckled[72]

With festering[73]

Black

Dots

Ever notice

In the midst of your weary[74] dreams

How fake I seem to be

Always freckled

---

[71] Shambles: a feeling of complete disorder
[72] Speckled: dotted
[73] Festering: rotting
[74] Weary: tired emotionally/dazed

With festering

Dark

Spots

I think it's called hiding

This thing that I am doing

Hiding from the heart

That would burden us all

If I deemed[75]

To learn

To feel

Again

Just words

Useless words

Wallowing[76]

Pity

Somber[77]

Guilt

Maybe something

---

[75] Deemed: decided
[76] Wallowing: letting yourself feel unrestrained emotion of a kind
[77] Somber: sadness

A bit like

Pandemonium[78]

Is crashing down

Perhaps I feel

The overwhelming hole

Of *lonely*

I hope

We're not

In this

Together

For if

We are

Then the world

Is burning

Straight down

To fucking

Hell.

---

[78] Pandemonium: complete chaos to the highest degree

FOR YOU

My heart is locked inside a safe

Tucked away till better days

It seems illogical why I'm afraid

But some things I'm just not ready to face

And I live for you

I'll stay for you

I'll be okay for you

My guilt

My anger

My fear locked away

Until it's not

Until I'm not

I'll live.

We're doomed to die

I'll stay.

My choice is gone

I'll be okay

Until I'm not

You know I'm not.

GRAY HAZE

Be the sunshine on cloudy days

Shine through as bright as a star

But how do you manage

On such cloudy days?

Let me tell you

It's with grace

But she's since slipped away

C'mon

What's so bad

About a little gray haze

I think I'll smile back to you

Whilst I fade

Remember me

Please?

To Say No

My heart is desolate[79]

And I am alone

For each breath I take

It gets harder and harder

For your sake

To say

No

And my heart is suffocating

Suffocating

From being left

All alone

---

[79] Desolate: away from people and with great emptiness

SACRIFICE

I'm tiring of asking

To sacrifice identity

Of

What am I willing to give up?

It's always something

Two years

Of drowning in the waves

Of my sorrow[80]

I'm tired

I am tired.

So what am I willing to give up?

There's not much more

Left to give

What am I willing

To give up?

Apparently

Everything.

---

[80] Sorrow: sadness

MISSING A FRIEND

I miss you

Dearly[81]

I can't make you

Hear me

But I'll say it anyway

Because

How else can I cope[82]

When all I've been doing is

Sitting here

Losing hope

Lately

You've been

Swirling around

In my head

And it's

Driving me insane

---

[81] Dearly: very much
[82] Cope: to manage your emotions well when something difficult happens in life

Such pandemonium

That is

My mind

Tell me when you could remember

The last time that you could breathe

Tell me how long it'd been since you

Last truly lived free

It's been years and I've got nowhere

It seems I'm all alone

I'm just counting days till I'll be

At long last

Overwhelmed

If death is fate

Then we'll fade away

Together

I said I was done

But we know that's not true

Till you curl[83] up to greet

The life anew[84]

---

[83] Curl: curve
[84] Anew: new, usually used in positive context

It feels good to cry

But the end is nigh

And I'll not spend my days in tears

It goes against my brain

And all that is sane

But I really

Wish you were here

I'm going insane

I can't take much more pain

What'll it take

What'll it take

For it all

To be over

I reach out and you're not there

Do you know how it feels

To grip phantom[85] air

Maybe I'm already broken

Maybe I'm already gone

---

[85] Phantom: something thought to be real, but was imagined

And I'll

Break

Down

Could you

Hear me

My sanity

Leaves me

I wish

I wish

That you

Were here

I wish

But wishes

Won't get me

Anywhere

But hey

All good things

End

But I had thought

We'd just

Began

But I wonder

Will I see sunshine

Again

Will I

See sunshine

Again

I REMEMBER...

I remember the good days

I remember your voice

Calling out to me

I wonder

How long will it take

Before mine fades from you

You once said

I could shine away the clouds

But the shadows are rolling in

And I'm breaking down

Tell me can you see it?

The world's end

I can see but all I want

Is a hug

From a friend

DISCONNECTION

I've been unplugged

Disconnected

From you

I want to be electrocuted

At least it's something I knew

Anything's better than being stranded

Alone

In a world of gray hues[86]

Pinpricked[87] by yellow

---

[86] Hues: shades of a color
[87] Pinpricked: spotted, usually used with context of pain

I WANT

I want to dance in the moonlight

I want the wind running through my hair

I want to pull the stars

Into my hand

So long as you'll be there

Maybe I want you to hold my hand

Maybe your presence[88] helps me to stand

Maybe you're the only thing

Blocking my fall

If it's truly the end

Maybe I just want a friend

Who was there

For it all

---

[88] Presence: being there

LONE WOLF

I'm a lone[89] wolf

From my pack I've long since strayed

I hunt alone

I run alone

But still

Its memory haunts[90] my ways

But a memory

I'll protect

Lest my life starts to fade

And I'm dead

As dead

Can be

I'm alone, wolf

Won't my pack come out to play?

---

[89] Lone: by itself
[90] Haunts: the act of constantly thinking of something

A HUG

Stuck

Inevitable[91] betrayal

Counting down days till

Pandemonium

All I want

Need

Is a hug

From a friend

Someone who understands

SO LONG

It's been so long

A month

Since you made contact

Two

Since I heard your voice

A year

Since things were normal

Maybe another

Until they will be again

It's been so long

And when I felt

Such rage, sorrow, longing[92] and grief

I kept my heart

Under lock and key

Reducing that heart to apathy[93]

Until you remembered me

And I forgot that cage

---

[92] Longing: wanting for something
[93] Apathy: the absence of emotion

That sorrow

That rage

And I wept[94]

I wept

Of joy

NOT ALONE

Anger, sadness, joy and tears

None can appear yet solo[95]

I'm not alone

But in the midst[96]

Of emptiness

In the longing ache[97] of silence

Your joy is all just white noise[98]

To me

It's just quiet monotony[99]

A fallen monarchy[100]

I'm not even in control of

My delusionality[101]

Anymore

Can't say I like reality

Any better

Though

---

[95] Solo: alone
[96] Midst: presence of
[97] Ache: pang
[98] White noise: background noise
[99] Monotony: boring-ness
[100] Monarchy: A system of government with kings and queens
[101] Delusionality: insanity

OVERWHELMED

I suffocated

Then burned

Later I drowned

Now I'm freezing

Soon I'll shatter

Ever wonder how it feels

Waiting

To be overwhelmed

WORST FEELING

What is the worst feeling

That one can hope to feel

Grief burns

Numbness[102] is cold

And the waves of lonely

Drown you in its allure[103]

But which

Which is worst

Perhaps you'll never know

You never can be sure

Unless

You've felt

Them all

And Godspeed[104]

Godspeed

To the unfortunate soul

To have been burdened so much

---

[102] Numbness: apathy
[103] Allure: a drawing in of
[104] Godspeed: a term for saying 'God be with you'

That if decided

They'd not utter a word

'Cause it hurts

And it's the closest yearn[105]

You'll ever feel

To just

Wanting

To give up

But power through

Don't dwell[106] on the past

Look to the future

Even if it's a future

To me

Left so unsure

---

[105] Yearn: overwhelming want
[106] Dwell: focus

INSPIRATION

So quiet

Such silence

Astounds[107] me

How could I

Bear this

Today

If I'm to

Suffer

Through this

How should I

Find

My joy

You see

It's hard

To conjure[108]

A smidgen

Of heart

---

[107] Astounds: surprises
[108] Conjure: make, sometimes used with spells

And

Inspiration

To pour to this

Lest you count

My soul's intrepid[109]

Blackness

ANUBIS'S SCALE[110]

If I were to die right now

I'd surely be one of the damned[111]

For whose heart weighs less than a feather

When they truly live for another

I've been bathed in holy water

There's many I would die for

My heart has been touched with Christ

So don't get me wrong when I say

That if I were to die today

My soul would find its way to hell

My heart would tip the scale Anubis holds

Bore[112] with the weight of secrets untold

---

[110] Anubis's Scale: a scale used by the Egyptian god of death to determine your afterlife by seeing if your heart weighs less than a feather
[111] Damned: people sent to Hell
[112] Bore: held up weight

MINT ICE CREAM

I want to

Curl into a ball

Around my violin

Like a little girl's doll

Mint speckling my tongue

So sweet

And cry

Myself

To sleep

I want you to hold tight

To me

So I can believe

It's more than just me

Alive

MUSIC

My music

Wonderfully done

My rhythm

Drifting[113] slowly

Down

My tether[114] to the Earth

Yet still pulling me

Drifting up to the clouds

A contradicting conundrum[115]

Of existence

I'm lost without my tethers

And one's already frayed[116]

I don't want to be in flux[117]

But hey!

Maybe it isn't so bad

Going mad

---

[113] Drifting: slowly falling
[114] Tether: rope/tie
[115] Conundrum: problem
[116] Frayed: the strings splitting apart on a rope's end
[117] Flux: a state of disorder

LOST

I wade[118] through seas of mud

Lost among the waves

It's growing more bothersome

Holding up this facade[119]

It's for your sake

But I'm starting to wonder

What'll become of me?

'Cause I'm so lost

In my listless[120] train of thought

Afraid of being consumed

And I can only think of two

Capable of rescue

Yet both

Lacking the courage to try

---

[118] Wade: walk slowly through a liquid
[119] Facade: an act that is not being true to yourself
[120] Listless: without direction

SHADES OF GRAY

I've spent the past years

Fumbling[121] through a haze

Wading through the swamps

Of such lovely shades of gray

If I ignore it all

Can I make it go away?

And when I'm asleep

My troubles are a dream

Such recurring[122] disappointment

Isn't healthy

You see

But when I wake

Truly wake

From my haunting

Shades of gray

I am blinded

I am blinded

By all the black

That I see

---

[121] Fumbling: walking clumsily
[122] Recurring: coming back over and over

COME HITHER

I've a lump in my throat

From a laugh or a cry

Maybe both; I'm not sure

I've long since blurred

Those lines

At this point it's pointless

These quarrels[123] of yours

So come hither[124]

Come hither

And join me

For the end of the world

---

[123] Quarrels: fights
[124] Hither: over here

EPILOGUE

*"Hold fast to dreams, for if dreams die,
life is a broken-winged bird that cannot fly."*

–Langston Hughes

DREAMER

I dream of stars

Above the moonlit clouds

A starry night where everything's right

And I can smile to the sky

I dream of sunsets

Surrounded by those I love

Where even if it's not easy I can find peace;

Find solace[125] in my heart

I dream of music

Carrying me away

Fantastic flits[126] of stardom

Where spirits are always raised

I dream of words

Scattered across a page

Cheers for when my dreams are shared

Wonder gone ablaze[127]

---

[125] Solace: peace/fulfillment
[126] Flits: short playful actions
[127] Ablaze: lit up

And I dream of storm clouds

Thunder booming down

The world turned dark grayish

Smiles turned to frowns

For I dream of twisted dreams

Ambitions[128] gone awry[129]

A dystopian[130] world of futures squandered[131]

And all that is left is to try

You don't have to be six feet under

To have a mountain on your back

You don't have to have anxiety

To be nervous it's all gonna crack

So I'll dream of sunsets

Of stars, the world abound

And I'll dare to dream of lightning

Dare to smile at the clouds

---

[128] Ambitions: dreams for the future
[129] Awry: wrong
[130] Dystopian: describes a future with certain things very bad or off in it
[131] Squandered: crushed

For when the storm hits

Whether I'll have that or starry skies

Whether our changing world will turn deranged

Or if my future will dare to shine

No matter the next landslide

That life will surely bring

I'll always be a dreamer

And that will *never* change.

Acknowledgements

On Optimism appeared first in Saint Andrew's 2021 poetry contest anthology collection, *Poetry in a Time of Pandemic* (published 2021, St. Andrew's Episcopal Church, First Edition) for the first place prize in the youth category.

Faith appeared first in Saint Andrew's 2021 poetry contest anthology collection, *Poetry in a Time of Pandemic* (published 2021, St. Andrew's Episcopal Church, First Edition).

ABOUT ATMOSPHERE PRESS

Atmosphere Press is an independent, full-service publisher for excellent books in all genres and for all audiences. Learn more about what we do at atmospherepress.com.

We encourage you to check out some of Atmosphere's latest releases, which are available at Amazon.com and via order from your local bookstore:

Until the Kingdom Comes, poetry by Jeanne Lutz

Warcrimes, poetry by GOODW.Y.N

The Freedom of Lavenders, poetry by August Reynolds

Convalesce, poetry by Enne Zale

Poems for the Bee Charmer (And Other Familiar Ghosts), poetry by Jordan Lentz

Serial Love: When Happily Ever After... Isn't, poetry by Kathy Kay

Flowers That Die, poetry by Gideon Halpin

Through The Soul Into Life, poetry by Shoushan B

Embrace The Passion In A Lover's Dream, poetry by Paul Turay

Reflections in the Time of Trumpius Maximus, poetry by Mark Fishbein

Drifters, poetry by Stuart Silverman

As a Patient Thinks about the Desert, poetry by Rick Anthony Furtak

Winter Solstice, poetry by Diana Howard

Blindfolds, Bruises, and Break-Ups, poetry by Jen Schneider

Songs of Snow and Silence, poetry by Jen Emery

INHABITANT, poetry by Charles Crittenden

Godless Grace, poetry by Michael Terence O'Brien

ABOUT THE AUTHOR

Photo by Michelle Bixby

Myah Robbins is a 15-year-old freshman who wrote this book, *One Perspective from the End of the World*, in years 13 and 14 of her life. In June of 2021, she won the youth category of Saint Andrew's *Poetry in a Time of Pandemic* poetry contest. Myah has been writing poetry consistently for two and a half years now, and she lives in a family of eight. Myah enjoys playing violin as well as writing and hopes to write more books in the future.

Made in the USA
Middletown, DE
19 September 2022